I0875959

GREEK MYTHOLOGY

ARES,
God of War

BY JOANNA BLAIR

Enslow PUBLISHING

Please visit our website, www.enslow.com. For a free color catalog of all our high-quality books, call toll free 1-800-398-2504 or fax 1-877-980-4454.

Cataloging-in-Publication Data
Names: Blair, Joanna.
Title: Ares, god of war / Joanna Blair.
Description: Buffalo, NY : Enslow Publishing, 2027. | Series: Greek mythology | Includes glossary and index.
Identifiers: ISBN 9781978550834 (pbk.) | ISBN 9781978550841 (library bound) | ISBN 9781978550858 (ebook)
Subjects: LCSH: Ares (Greek deity)--Juvenile literature. | Mythology, Greek--Juvenile literature. | Gods, Greek--Juvenile literature.
Classification: LCC BL820.M2 B535 2027 | DDC 292.2113--dc23

Published in 2027 by
Enslow Publishing
2544 Clinton Street
Buffalo, NY 14224

Copyright © 2027 Enslow Publishing

Portions of this work were originally authored by Christine Ha and published as *Ares*. All new material in this edition was authored by Joanna Blair.

Cover Designer: Joshua Olson
Interior Designer: Joshua Olson
Editor: Claire Vanden Branden

Photo Credits: Cover, p. 1 Alexander Ruszczynski/Shutterstock.com; pp. 4–5 Panos Karas/Shutterstock.com; p. 6 kanvag/Shutterstock.com; pp. 7, 29 Pedro Helder Pinheiro/Shutterstock.com; pp. 8–9 Storm Is Me/Shutterstock.com; pp. 10–11 Chubykin Arkady/Shutterstock.com; pp. 12–13 Rijksmuseum; pp. 14–15 Tonello Photography/Shutterstock.com; pp. 16–17 ImagesGR/Shutterstock.com; p. 18 Renata Sedmakova/Shutterstock.com; p. 19 Michael Rosskothen/Shutterstock.com; pp. 20–21 The Posavje Museum Brežice; pp. 22–23 Lysogor Roman/Shutterstock.com; pp. 24–25 Epopsis/Shutterstock.com; pp. 26–27 Evgeny Shaparin/Shutterstock.com.

All rights reserved. No part of this book may be reproduced in any form without permission in writing from the publisher, except by a reviewer.

Printed in China

CPSIA compliance information: Batch #QS27ENS: For further information contact Enslow Publishing, at 1-800-398-2504.

Find us on

TABLE OF CONTENTS

CHAPTER 1

BORN TO BATTLE

Ares was the Greek god of war. He was the son of Zeus and Hera. Many stories say he was born in northeastern Greece.

Legends say Ares was born in Thrace. The land in this area was wild.

Ares was **violent**. He got angry quickly. He often started fights and battles.

Some Greek soldiers wore helmets with tall crests on the tops.

In art, Ares is often shown wearing a helmet.

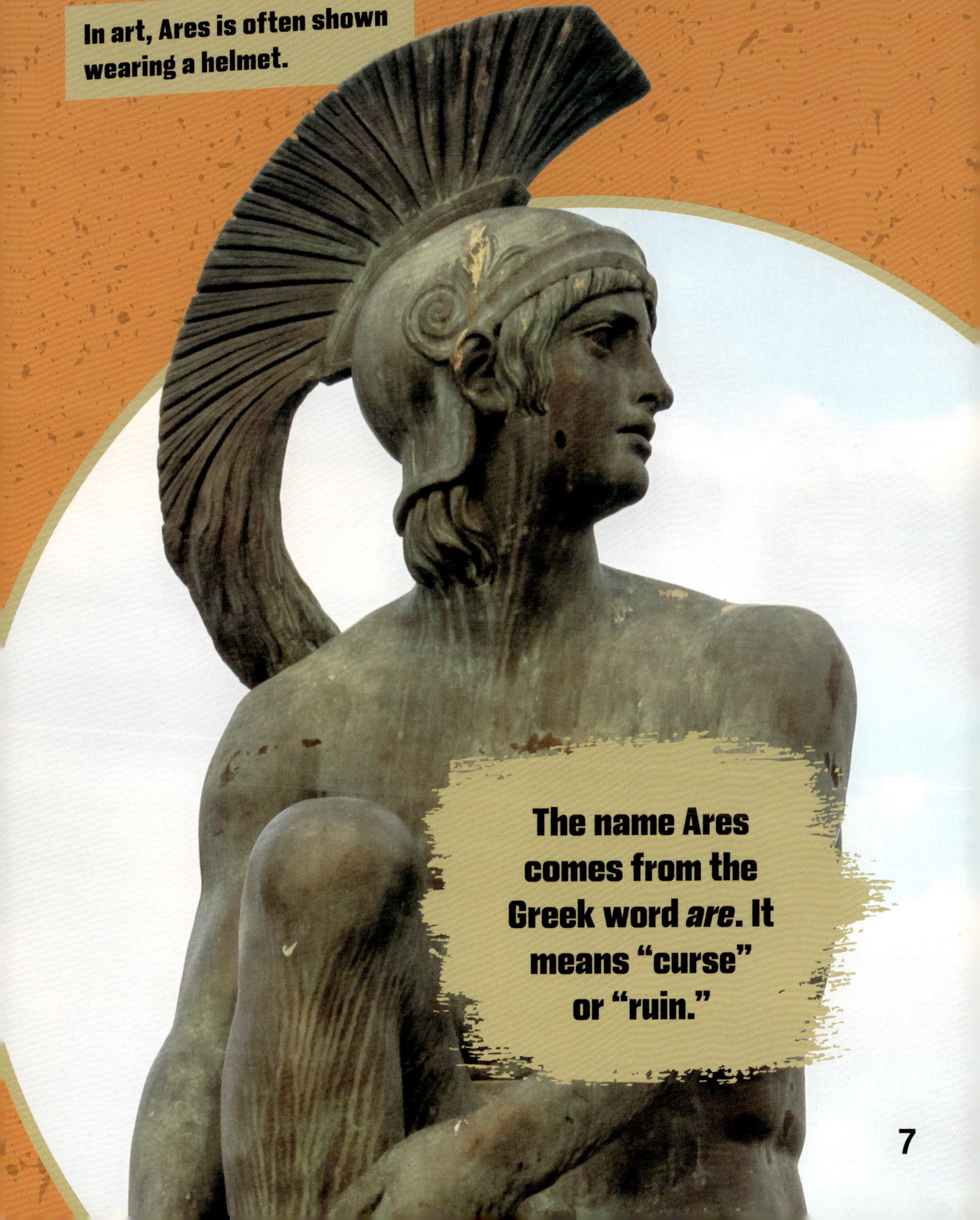

The name Ares comes from the Greek word *are*. It means "curse" or "ruin."

Ares rarely fought alone. His sons and sisters were often at his side. Deimos and Phobos were both gods of fear. Eris was the goddess of **strife**. The goddess Enyo steered Ares's **chariot**.

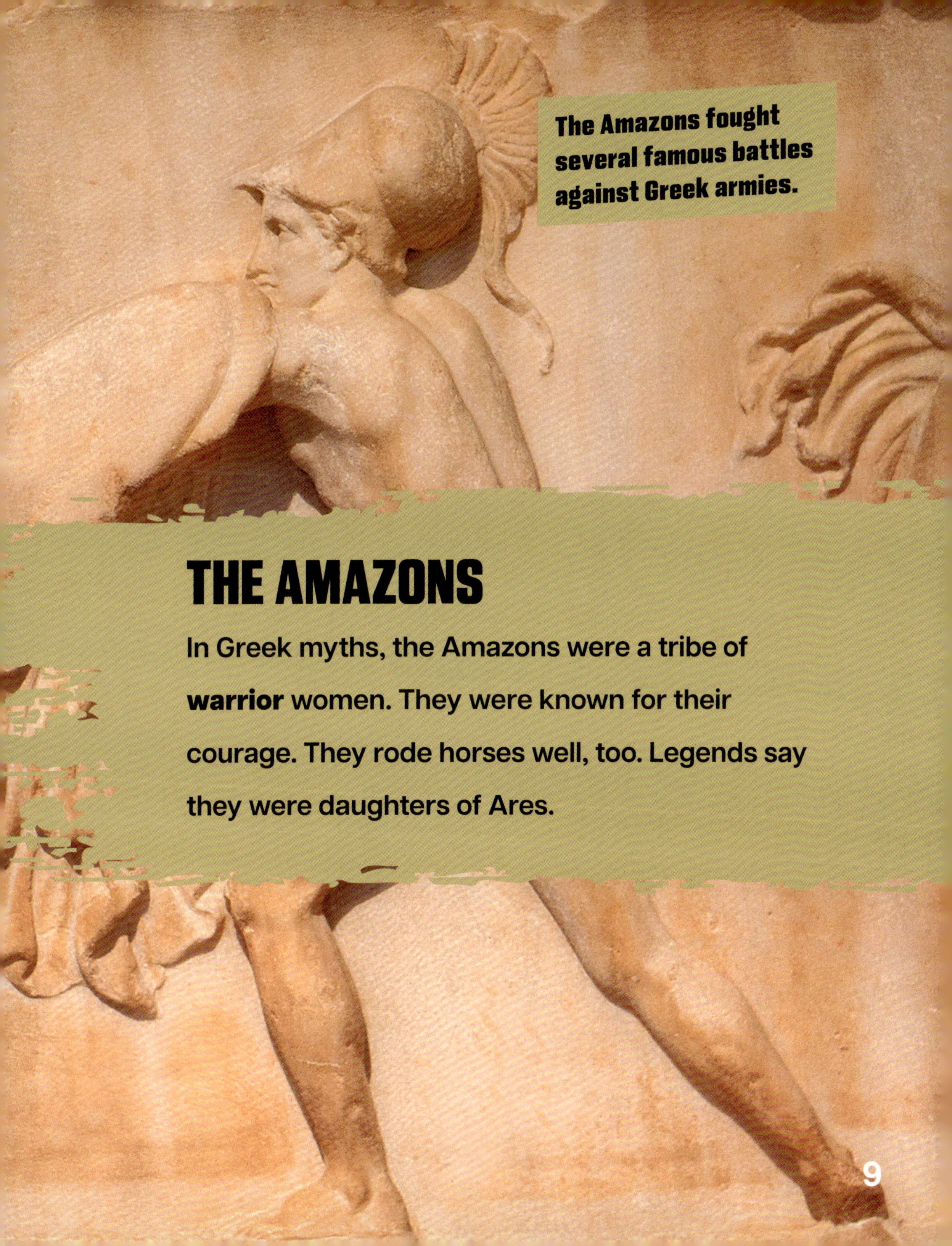

The Amazons fought several famous battles against Greek armies.

THE AMAZONS

In Greek myths, the Amazons were a tribe of **warrior** women. They were known for their courage. They rode horses well, too. Legends say they were daughters of Ares.

CHAPTER 2

ABOUT ARES

Ares was incredibly strong and fast. He could fight without getting tired. Ares was immortal. He could get hurt. But he could never die.

Heroes sometimes hurt Ares in fights. But they couldn't kill him.

Ares was always ready to ride into battle.

Ares rode through battles in his chariot. The noise of his horses running filled the sky. It was as loud as thunder.

ARES'S CHARIOT

Four black horses pulled Ares's chariot. The horses breathed fire. Wild dogs and vultures often followed Ares, too.

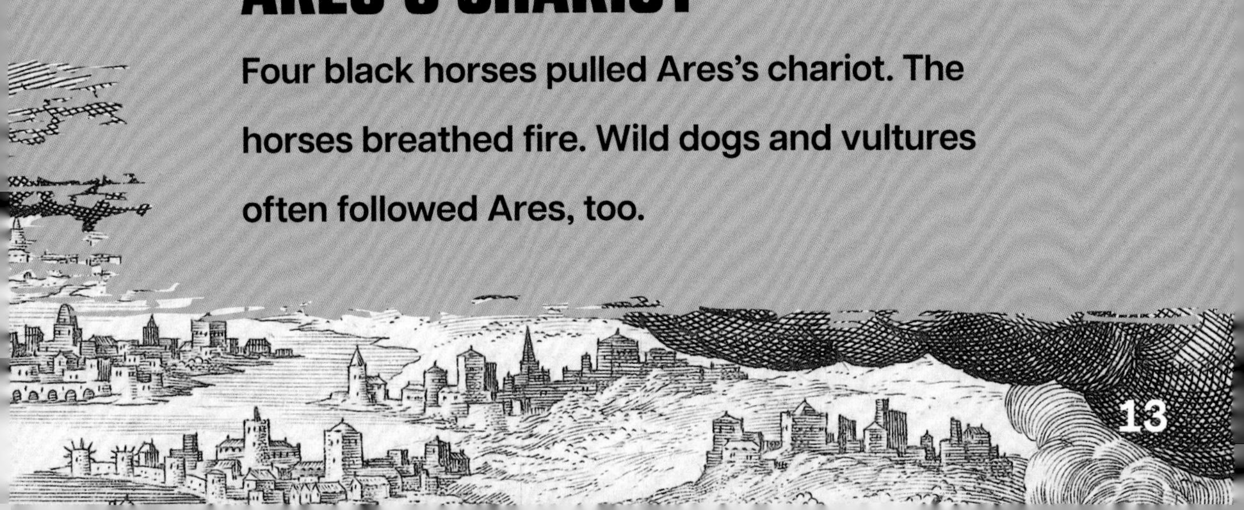

In one myth, two giants tried to fight the gods. Ares battled them. But they captured Ares instead. He was held in a jar for 13 months.

Ares usually fought with a spear and a shield. Sometimes he also had a sword.

Greek soldiers carried round shields.

CHAPTER 3

OUTSMARTED

Ares had great strength. But people sometimes beat him. They got help from the goddess Athena. She could outsmart Ares.

Athena was the goddess of wisdom. She often helped people win battles.

Athena often helped heroes fight Ares. For example, Ares tried to kill Hercules. But Athena kept the hero safe. He fought Ares and won.

In Greek myths, heroes often fought gods and monsters.

Ares and Athena helped opposite sides in the Trojan War. Athena's side won.

Athena helped the Greeks trick the Trojans. Soldiers hid inside a giant horse.

DIFFERENT STRENGTHS

Ares and Athena were both gods of war. They controlled different parts of fighting. Ares liked force and violence. Athena focused on **strategy** and skill.

Athena beat Ares in many stories. These stories showed the Greeks' **values**. They showed that intelligence was better than force.

Mars was the Roman version of Ares. He was one of Rome's main gods.

Ares was one of the 12 main Greek gods.

CHAPTER 4

ARES'S POWER

Many Greeks didn't like Ares. He was often angry. And he was **destructive**. These traits made him unpopular. Few people prayed to him.

The Roman god Mars was much more popular than the Greek god Ares.

Ares was mostly worshipped in northern Greece. He was especially popular in Sparta and Thebes. These cities had strong armies. They **admired** Ares's power.

Spartan boys began training to be soldiers at age seven.

Some Greek cities built fortresses for protection.

Part of one temple for Ares still stands in the city of Athens.

Ares did have a few temples. They often stood outside of cities. People placed them there for protection. They thought Ares would stop enemies from getting in.

A NEW HOME

The Greeks built a famous temple for Ares in an area called Pallene near Athens. The Romans took this temple apart. They moved it to Athens and rebuilt it there stone by stone.

TEST YOUR KNOWLEDGE

Take this quiz to test your knowledge.

1. Write a few sentences explaining the main ideas of Chapter 4.
2. Would you want Ares to be on your side in a fight? Why or why not?
3. Which goddess did Ares often fight against?
   - A. Eris
   - B. Enyo
   - C. Athena
4. How were the Amazons similar to Ares?
   - A. They were skilled fighters.
   - B. They were calm and peaceful.
   - C. They were sons of Zeus.

5. What does **immortal** mean in this book?

Ares was ***immortal****. He could get hurt. But he could never die.*

A. able to know everything
B. able to live forever
C. not able to move

6. What does **captured** mean in this book?

But they ***captured*** *Ares instead. He was held in a jar for 13 months.*

A. caught someone
B. lost someone
C. let someone go

Answers can be found on page 32.

GLOSSARY

admired
Liked or wanted to be like someone or something.

chariot
A two-wheeled cart pulled by horses or other animals.

destructive
Causing lots of damage.

strategy
Careful planning to solve a problem or reach a goal.

strife
Feelings or fights that are bitter and angry.

values
Beliefs about what is good or important.

violent
Likely to use physical force to hurt or attack.

warrior
A brave person who has fought many battles.

FOR MORE INFORMATION

BOOKS

Buckey, A. W. *Greek Mythology Gods.* San Diego, CA: BrightPoint Press, 2022.

Lock, Deborah. *Greek Myths.* New York, NY: DK Publishing, 2023.

WEBSITES

Britannica Kids: Greek Mythology

kids.britannica.com/kids/article/Greek-mythology/598932

Read more myths about Greek gods at this website.

National Geographic: The Gods and Goddesses of Ancient Greece!

natgeokids.com/nz/discover/history/greece/greek-gods

Learn more about Greek gods and goddesses.

Publisher's note to educators and parents: Our editors have carefully reviewed these websites to ensure that they are suitable for students. Many websites change frequently, however, and we cannot guarantee that a site's future contents will continue to meet our high standards of quality and educational value. Be advised that students should be closely supervised whenever they access the internet.

INDEX

Answer Key:
1. Answers will vary; 2. Answers will vary; 3. C; 4. A; 5. B; 6. A